HERITAGE UN

Guide to free sites in

Hardknott Roman Fort, Cumbria

CONTENTS

Published by English Heritage, 23 Savile Row, London W1S 2ET.

First published by English Heritage 2002.
Edited by Sarah Yates. Designed by Pauline Hull.
Print production by Richard Jones. Printed in England by Empress.
C80 12/02 02198 ISBN 1 85074 831 4

As well as major attractions such as Beeston and Carlisle castles, the North West contains a wealth of English Heritage sites to which entry is free. This new guidebook, the first in a planned series, provides a concise but informative introduction to each of these sites, in Cheshire, Cumbria and Lancashire. The diversity of these sites reflects the long, varied and often turbulent history of this region. Among the earliest are the mysterious monuments of Castlerigg Stone Circle, King Arthur's Round Table and Mayburgh Henge, which may have been used for social, ritual or trading activities by prehistoric communities. During the period of Roman occupation, the region served as the empire's northernmost frontier, as demonstrated by such impressive monuments as Hadrian's Wall – extending from Wallsend in the east to Maryport in the west – and the forts at Ambleside, Hardknott and Ravenglass. The strategic importance of the North West, on the border of England and Scotland, continued throughout the medieval period: such monuments as Penrith Castle were built to defend the towns from raids by the Scots. The imposing remains of castles and abbeys also reflect the wealth and power of both the monastic orders and dominant landholding families such as the Cliffords. The later strong local tradition of religious nonconformism is evident in buildings of later centuries, such as Goodshaw Chapel. Throughout the book are features highlighting some aspects of the region's history and character, such as its significant industrial heritage, and its landscape as a continuing source of inspiration for British artists and writers. This book aims to encourage visitors to explore, understand and enjoy some of the lesser-known but intriguing monuments in English Heritage's care.

Industry has had an enormous impact on the North West, and the region's natural resources were exploited from the earliest times. Stone axes, made in the Langdale area, were traded across Europe in the Neolithic period. The Romans mined lead in the Lake District, iron in the Furness peninsula, and copper and salt in Cheshire.

In the medieval period mining in the region became increasingly sophisticated: from the twelfth century, the monks of Furness Abbey exploited the local iron reserves, while lead was mined in the Lake District and on Alston Moor. The silver found in association with the lead was extracted by smelting, fuelled by peat, charcoal, and later coal and coke. Later barytes, copper, tungsten and zinc were also mined. From the eighteenth century gunpowder mills were built in the Lake District to supply the explosives used in mining and quarrying. Many of these industries depended on water power, which also drove corn mills all over the region.

The North West was the heartland of the Industrial Revolution. While the first steps towards industrialisation were taken elsewhere, it was here that the most intensive development occurred. It was based around textiles, although the region also became known for other manufactures, among them chemicals, iron and steel. Other industries developed to service the cotton mills, while canals and, later, railways were built to supply them with fuel and to transport finished goods. Coal was mined in Lancashire to power the mills, and in west Cumbria to fuel the developing iron and steel

Viaduct across the Sankey Valley, 1831, from the Liverpool and Manchester Railway *series of engravings by Henry Pyall*

industry. Liverpool became the country's largest port outside London, importing raw cotton from America and India, and exporting the finished textiles all over the world. Old towns expanded and new ones developed to house the industrial workers.

Much of this industry disappeared in the twentieth century. Most textile mills are now redundant, and many have been demolished. The last coal mines closed more than twenty years ago, while lead mining in the Lake District and on Alston Moor had largely ended by the Second World War. Most of Liverpool's docks are now disused, and many former industrial towns are now classed as depressed areas.

Yet the buildings, monuments and landscapes that remain from the region's industrial past are now recognised as internationally important. Two of the areas proposed for World Heritage Site status, the port of Liverpool and the Ancoats, Castlefield and Worsley corridor, were important centres of the Industrial Revolution.

English Heritage engages with the North West's industrial heritage in a variety of ways. Surveys of individual sites, areas or groups of sites relating to the same industry ('thematic' surveys) identify industrial remains, record what survives and provide essential information for their management. Recent surveys of individual towns, or parts of them, are aimed at understanding their development and preserving their essential character. The most important buildings and sites are put forward for legal protection. This may prevent a building or site from being deliberately destroyed but cannot alone ensure its survival. No single agency can hope to preserve the vast collection of industrial buildings and monuments that are so characteristic of the North West. Partnership – with other government agencies, local authorities, local trusts and the Heritage Lottery Fund – is the key to finding new uses for redundant industrial buildings, which will give them a viable future.

Converted warehouse, in Princess Street, Manchester

CHESHIRE

The legacy of the Roman Empire is still evident in Cheshire today, especially in the city of Chester: founded by the Romans about AD 48, it contains the remains of Britain's largest Roman amphitheatre. From the Norman Conquest until the sixteenth century Cheshire was a feudal province with its own parliament, and Chester was a base for Edward I's conquest of Wales. Its connection with royalty continued in later centuries: the city was the head-quarters of Royalist forces during the Civil War, until it surrendered in 1646. The county is largely agricultural, but salt has been mined here since Roman times, while Macclesfield and Congleton became renowned as centres of silk weaving.

***Opposite**: The Sandbach Crosses*

***Below left**: Remains of the Roman amphitheatre at Chester*

***Below**: Roman fresco from Pompeii showing a fight in an amphitheatre*

Description

Chester Castle lies in the south-west part of the walled city. In the Middle Ages it consisted of an outer bailey – remodelled at the beginning of the nineteenth century – and an inner bailey. All the remaining medieval parts lie in what was formerly the inner bailey, reached through an archway at the far right-hand corner of the parade ground.

In the inner bailey, the imposing building in front of you is Napier House, built in 1830 as an armoury and barracks. On your left is the Guardroom, housing a display on the history of the castle. Behind it stands the twelfth-century Agricola Tower, the original gateway to the castle; the blocked passage arch is still visible. On its first floor is the chapel of St Mary de Castro, which contains the remains of some very high-quality wall paintings of about 1240. The heavy, copper-plated door dates from the early nineteenth century, when the chapel was used as a gunpowder store.

By leaving the tower and climbing the stairs onto the walls, you can appreciate the location of the castle within the city. Below, to your left, is the Old Dee Bridge, the traditional route into north Wales, and around to your right is the Roodee, the silted-up port area of Chester. Behind Napier House is a gun platform, built for defence in 1745 in response to the Jacobite rising of Bonnie Prince Charlie. Note the steps leading down to the sally port.

Continue to the top of the ramp that leads back down into the

The medieval Chester walls

courtyard of the inner bailey. This raised area incorporates the Norman 'motte' or mound of the original castle (best viewed from outside the castle). To your left, on the site of the original keep, stands the square medieval Flag Tower. The white-painted building beside it is the Frobisher's or Furbisher's House, named after the officer charged with overseeing the storage of weapons at the castle.

History

Chester Castle was founded by William the Conqueror in 1070 and became the administrative centre of the Earldom of Chester. The first earth and timber 'motte and bailey' castle probably only occupied the area of the inner bailey. In the twelfth century it was rebuilt in stone and the outer bailey added. In 1237 the last earl died and the castle, with the earldom, was taken over by the king. In 1265, during the Barons' War, it was held for ten weeks by supporters of Simon de Montfort against the men of Prince Edward, son of Henry III.

The Agricola Tower entrance

During the reigns of Henry III and Edward I the castle served as the military headquarters for the conquest of Wales and much building was carried out, especially in the outer bailey. In the later medieval period the monarch rarely stayed at the castle, but it continued to serve as the centre for county administration. During the Civil War (1642–6) it was the head-quarters of the Royalist governor, John, Lord Byron. Subsequently a permanent garrison was stationed there, and between 1788 and 1813 the outer bailey was completely rebuilt in the Neo-classical style. The buildings still serve as the county hall, courts and regimental museum, but the military finally withdrew in 1999.

Access via Assizes Court car park on Grosvenor Street
OS Map 117; ref SJ 404657
Agricola Tower: Open 29 Mar-30 Sep: 10am-5pm daily; 1 Oct-31 Mar: 10am-4pm daily; closed 24-26 Dec and 1 Jan

Before the Roman conquest of Britain in AD 43, much of northern England was controlled by the tribe of the Brigantes, whose chief centres appear to have been in and to the east of the Pennines (at Stanwick and Barwick-in-Elmet) and in the North West (near Brougham). By the 40s AD the Roman empire had treaties with the Brigantian leaders Cartimandua and Venutius, which ensured that the North remained essentially peaceful.

In AD 69, however, Venutius drove Cartimandua from power, and the Roman military response came in the form of attacks mounted by three governors – Bolanus (69–71), Cerialis (71–4) and Agricola (77–83). Their land assaults from the north-west Midlands crossed the plains of Cheshire and Lancashire and followed the valleys of the Lune and Eden to Carlisle, one of the earliest and most significant forts in the region; these were accompanied by naval landings by troops from the Dee Estuary. Roman campaign camps from this period have mostly been obliterated by ploughing, although some remains may still be seen in the Pennines and at Troutbeck (by the A66, near Keswick).

In the late 80s the frontier of the Roman province was established between the Tyne and the Solway, first by the fortified road known as the Stanegate, and in the 120s by Hadrian's Wall. Such frontiers were not intended to prevent movement into and out of the province, but to regulate it for political and fiscal purposes. Hadrian's Wall also demonstrated Rome's technological and organisational superiority, as well as being an enduring monument to the Emperor Hadrian. Eventually the

Hadrian's Wall running eastwards from Birdoswald to Harrow's Scar is the longest visible stretch of the Wall rebuilt in stone late in Hadrian's reign

frontier extended from Wallsend on the River Tyne to Maryport on the Cumbrian coast. The hinterland of the Wall was policed by a network of forts (including those at Ambleside, Hardknott and Ravenglass). Other sites such as Warrington and Heronbridge (near Chester) were dedicated to manufacturing and commerce.

A coin from the reign of Hadrian showing a Roman warship

Military conquest was not an end in itself; it was intended to provide the conditions in which the native population co-operated with the Romans to create a cosmopolitan, Romanised British society. For Rome this approach was far cheaper and easier than having to deploy large numbers of troops to control a recalcitrant local population. The soldiers' wealth encouraged people to settle close to the forts and to benefit by providing a range of services and consumer goods; hence small towns, such as Manchester, developed outside almost every fort. Business thrived, and one north-west town – Carlisle – eventually became the regional administrative centre for the Romanised tribe of the Carvetii.

There was also good-quality agricultural land in the North West, especially on the Solway Plain and in the river valleys. Through mainly aerial survey, Roman farms of diverse plan and size have been located; they belonged to former soldiers and to local people making their living from supplying the military garrisons and associated civilians. The remains of such sites survive in the region's more remote areas.

As the empire declined in the fourth and fifth centuries some of the local population organised themselves into militia-groups under 'warlords' (such as the semi-legendary Arthur) to defend this Romano-British culture; they also tried to maintain the buildings constructed under Roman rule – with some success, as Carlisle's water system, still operating in the seventh century, testified. Eventually, however, the Roman influence declined, and their forts and other buildings fell into decay.

An altar found at Maryport on the coastal extension to Hadrian's Wall, dedicated to Jupiter by Marcus Maenius Agrippa

Chester Roman Amphitheatre was built in the late first century AD, when many such buildings were being constructed throughout the Roman Empire. It lay just outside the south-east corner of the Roman legionary fortress, and was probably used both for entertainments and for practising troop manoeuvres and weapon training.

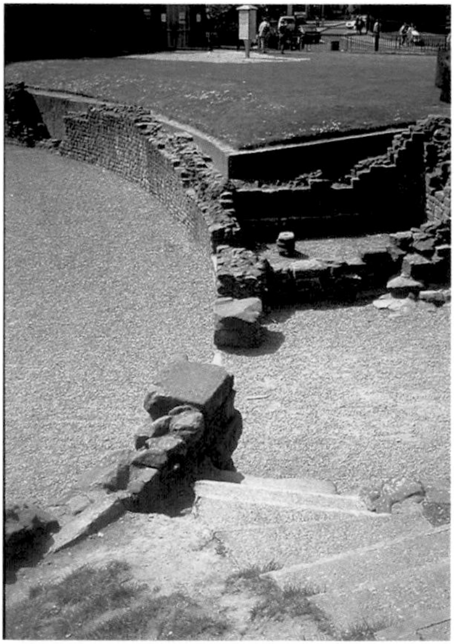

The north entrance to the amphitheatre, with the shrine to Nemesis

Only about two-fifths of the oval amphitheatre is visible; the rest lies unexcavated behind the brick wall. In the excavated part, two entrances have been exposed: the larger lies on the long axis to the north, while the smaller lies on the short axis to the east. Lining the arena is the original stone wall, although, owing to later removal, some sections are missing and there is modern concrete backing.

Excavations in the 1960s suggested that the building was originally constructed entirely of wood, but further archaeological investigation in 2001 cast doubt on this theory. The stone structure seen today had an outer wall 9 ft (2.7 m) thick, marked out by concrete slabs set in the grass. Inside it ran a corridor linking the entrances that led to stairways taking the spectators up into the seating area. The two entrances visible today were used by the performers; their sloping floors show that the arena floor was sunk over 3 ft (1 m) below Roman ground level. Just inside the corridor of the north entrance is a set of stairs, which led to a small room housing the officials who controlled activities in the arena.

Inside the arena was a small door to the left of the north entrance. The room behind it contained an altar dedicated to the goddess Nemesis, who was believed to control the fate of the performers. In most amphitheatres, these shrines were outside the arena; perhaps some performances in Chester included a visit to it.

The amphitheatre did not enjoy a long initial period of use: by the 120s AD it had become derelict and was being used as a rubbish dump. This happened around the time that the Twentieth Legion was posted north to help build Hadrian's Wall. It was not until about AD 275 that it was brought back into use, when new paving was laid inside the arena, the shrine to Nemesis was refurbished and a colonnade was inserted in the east entrance. It remained as a functioning amphitheatre until finally being abandoned about AD 350.

The Colosseum in Rome, the model for all Roman amphitheatres

During the fifth or sixth century there may have been a timber hall in the arena, standing for long enough to need rebuilding. Later the large blocks in the east entrance were inserted. On one side it is still possible to see the very worn steps that led down into this space, which was possibly built as the crypt of the original St John's Church in the seventh century. Most of the later history of the site is one of neglect and demolition: during the medieval period it was nothing more than a quarry for building stone and a convenient rubbish dump. By about 1200 houses had been built over it, and it was not until the 1950s that it was uncovered and later excavated.

On Vicars Lane beyond Newgate, Chester
OS Map 117; ref SJ 408661

SANDBACH CROSSES

Top: *View of the crosses at Sandbach* **Bottom:** *Detail of stone carving* **Opposite:** *Reconstruction drawing of the larger cross by Peter Dunn*

Market square, Sandbach

OS Map 118; ref SJ 758608

The two massive crosses standing in the market square at Sandbach are thought, from their iconography, to date back to the early ninth century. So fine is their carved decoration that they have prompted speculation that a minster or a monastery – with an associated workshop of skilled sculptors – was located at Sandbach during the Saxon period. Whether these sandstone crosses were an expression of the power of such an establishment, set up as boundary markers, or used in religious services is unclear. It is unlikely that they commemorate the introduction of Christianity into Mercia by King Peada in AD 643 (as the bronze plaque asserts). They are often described as being among the most important surviving examples of Anglo-Saxon high crosses.

Probably moved from their unknown original site to the market-place in the sixteenth century, the crosses have had an eventful history. They were violently broken up, probably by Puritans, in the seventeenth century and the pieces distributed around the vicinity (and even incorporated into an artificial grotto at Oulton). In 1816 they were reassembled and re-erected; some other Anglo-Saxon stone fragments remain by the porch of St Mary's Church.

The decoration on the larger cross focuses on biblical subjects. Among the carved narrative scenes is a Nativity with a Crucifixion above it, an Adoration of the Magi and an Annunciation. A luxuriant vine scroll appears on the south side. The figures, animals and ornament on the smaller cross are more difficult to interpret, although they most likely represent different aspects of the Christian community.

CUMBRIA

The second largest county in England, Cumbria contains some of the country's most spectacular scenery, in particular the mountains, lakes and moorland of the Lake District. Evidence of human activity since the earliest times is found in the numerous prehistoric monuments, such as Castlerigg Stone Circle, King Arthur's Round Table and Mayburgh Henge. During the Roman period roads and forts were constructed to protect settlements in the hinterland of Hadrian's Wall. The history of many medieval monuments is marked by the long battle for control of Cumbria between the Scots and English. However, from the eighteenth century their ruins inspired many writers and artists, notably William Wordsworth.

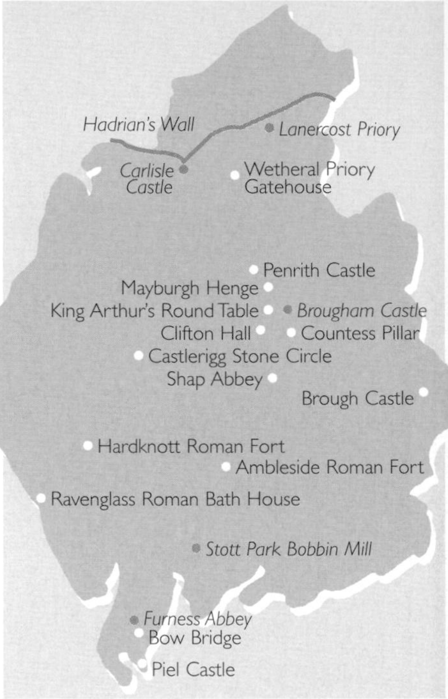

Opposite: *Hardknott Roman Fort*

Left: *Detail of Castlerigg Stone Circle from* The English Lake District, *1853, by James Baker Pyne*

Right: *Eighteenth-century drawing of Clifton Hall by Christopher Machell*

Aerial view of Ambleside Roman Fort, showing the central range of buildings and the edge of Lake Windermere in the bottom left corner

Description

The remains of the fort lie in Borrans Field, at the northern end of Lake Windermere. The entrance to the fort is through its main (east) gate, which had a double carriageway and flanking guard towers; in very dry weather, the line of the Roman road approaching the gate can be clearly seen as a crop-mark in the grass. Parts of the gates and sections of the fort walls are exposed, but the most significant surviving structures are the headquarters and granaries.

The headquarters building consisted of a courtyard flanked by rooms possibly used as armouries; beyond this was the 'cross-hall', a roofed extension of the courtyard and the centre of administration for the fort. To the rear of this was a small temple containing the military standards, beneath which was a sunken strong-room or treasury where the garrison's funds and the soldiers' savings were kept – the sanctity of the room above was thought sufficient to deter thieves. On either side of the temple were administrative offices.

To the right of the headquarters building were the two granaries. These were substantial in size – perhaps larger than required by this fort alone – suggesting that Ambleside may have functioned as a storage and distribution centre for regional supplies. The floor consisted of flagstones, raised on the still visible supporting walls to allow air to circulate through the vents in the outer walls.

To the left of the headquarters building are the partly excavated remains of the commander's residence, consisting of rooms grouped around an open courtyard. The large size of this building reflects the importance of the fort commander. The areas to the front and rear of the central range of buildings would have been occupied largely by barracks and perhaps stables.

History

Covering three acres, the fort was probably built during the reign of the Emperor Hadrian (AD 117–38). However, excavations have suggested the presence, partly beneath the stone buildings, of an earlier fort with a turf wall and timber buildings, constructed possibly in the 90s AD, when Roman control of the Lake District was being consolidated.

Little is known of the fort's history, and the identity of none of its garrisons has been established. A tombstone of Flavius Romanus from the third century, which was found in the 1960s to the east of the fort, states that he was killed by an enemy inside the fort; whether his killer was a personal enemy or a member of an attacking force is unknown. Finds suggest that the fort was occupied into the later fourth century and beyond. Given its strategic location, this fort, like that at Birdoswald on Hadrian's Wall, could have become the base for a local warlord and his militia after the Romans departed.

The most interesting theory regarding Ambleside is that it had a significant regional role in supplying the Roman troops who policed the Lake District. Its location, so close to Windermere, made it a suitable reception point for goods transported by ship. This suggestion is supported by the large size of the granaries and of the settlement outside the fort, which extended at least 875 yds (800 m) to the north.

Remains of the sunken treasury

200 yds (182 m) W of Waterhead car park, Ambleside
OS Map 90; ref NY 376033

BOW BRIDGE

Situated near Furness Abbey, Bow Bridge provides a convenient point at which to cross Mill Beck beside the sluice of a former mill race. Although not breathtaking in scale (being just 10 ft [3 m] wide), Bow is still a fine example of a three-arched medieval bridge. The stone parapets that probably ran along either side of the central footpath and gave the structure extra strength have now disappeared.

Bow Bridge was built in the fifteenth century from the same plentiful supply of red sandstone and grey limestone as Furness Abbey, which dates back to the 1120s. In its heyday Furness was the most powerful abbey in the North West and, at the time of the Dissolution of the Monasteries in the 1530s, the second richest Cistercian monastery in England. The surviving richly embellished arcades and the magnificently carved details bear witness to its wealth and importance.

Such a prosperous abbey cannot fail to have attracted merchants, traders and salesmen, as well as Scottish raiders. During the medieval period, the traffic to and from Furness must have been fast and furious, with Bow Bridge carrying a steady stream of pedestrians and pack-horses laden with corn, malt, salt and other goods. The bridge may have been constructed specifically to link the abbey with the nearby New Mill, but its position on one of the most important medieval trading routes in north-west England must surely be of even greater significance.

Bow Bridge

Located 1/2 mile N of Barrow-in-Furness on a minor road off A590 near Furness Abbey

OS Map 96; ref SD 224715

Description

Brough Castle was constructed on the site of the Roman fort of Verteris, one in a chain of forts guarding the road running from York over the Pennines to Carlisle. The castle's strong defensive position on a steep slope above Swindall Beck and its sturdy walls are eloquent reminders that, at the beginning of the twelfth century, this area of England was in constant danger of attack from the kings of Scotland.

As you approach the castle from the south east, along the road from Church Brough, you will see the square keep on your left, with the gatehouse straight ahead and the main fourteenth-century living quarters on your right. Two elegant, traceried windows mark the position of the great hall. On the extreme right is Clifford's Tower, the semicircular building completed about 1300 by Robert Clifford.

Pass through the gatehouse into the partially walled courtyard and begin your exploration of the castle by turning to your left. Walk past the stables (added in the late 1600s) towards the imposing keep. Built in the late twelfth century on the Norman masonry of an earlier tower, the keep was originally used for storage and shelter in times of siege. It was later converted by Lady Anne Clifford into guest accommodation, as can be seen from the fireplaces and the traces of plaster clinging to the inside walls.

8 miles SE of Appleby, S of A66
OS Map 91;
ref NY 791141

Previous page: Bird's-eye view painting of Brough Castle by Peter Dunn

Continue around the courtyard to the remains opposite the gatehouse. These are the foundations of the bakehouse, brewhouse and kitchen constructed by Lady Anne in 1661 as part of her campaign to improve the service quarters of all her castles.

Cross over to Clifford's Tower and the fragmentary structures clustered around it. Lady Anne's restorations were aesthetic as well as practical. Her aim seems to have been to bring Brough back to life as a Tudor castle. Her style, which has been labelled 'northern Gothic', is still visible in the rectangular windows of Clifford's Tower with their solid lintels and frames. The ground floor of the tower housed the laundress's room until the late seventeenth century, while the floors above contained chambers refurbished for Lady Anne herself.

Other buildings in this corner of the courtyard are the ruins of two parallel ranges, one built in the late fourteenth century against the south curtain wall and the other, set alongside the first, built in the mid-fifteenth century. Piercing the outer wall are the two medieval windows of the first-floor hall. Below the hall are three vaulted storerooms and the remains of the spiral staircase that led from the hall up to the great chamber, where the senior members of the household ate.

The gatehouse and keep

History

The oldest parts of the castle date back to about 1100, although these are just scanty traces since in 1174 William the Lion, King of Scotland, captured Brough and set it on fire: as a result almost the entire keep was destroyed. By the time King John gave Brough to Robert de Vieuxpont in 1203, a new keep had been built. Robert, who owned nearby Brougham Castle too, was a loyal supporter of the Crown and rebuilt the gatehouse. He may also have added some domestic buildings before the castle passed to the Cliffords in 1268.

Robert Clifford, who became one of the leading barons of his day, built a new hall and Clifford's Tower at the south-east end of the courtyard as a residence for himself and his family. Scottish attacks led to the strengthening of the curtain wall in 1314 and 1319. Brough experienced its greatest period of change in the hands of Roger Clifford, who completely altered the layout of the living quarters in the fourteenth century. The Cliffords seem to have spent much time at Brough, celebrating Christmas there with a great feast in 1521. Unfortunately fire broke out and devastated the whole castle, destroying floors, windows and doors.

Had it not been for the intervention of Lady Anne Clifford, the story of Brough might have ended there. She inherited the castle from her father, George, Earl of Cumberland, and in 1659 she took it in hand, making substantial additions (such as the stables) and lovingly restoring the damaged parts. After her death in 1676, Brough was neglected and allowed to decay: in 1763 the domestic wing was robbed of stone to repair Brough Mill. In 1920 the castle was placed in the guardianship of the Ministry of Works.

Lady Anne Clifford

The remains of Clifford's Tower

North West England, in particular its landscape, has long inspired British writers and painters. In the late eighteenth century the Gothic novelist Ann Radcliffe described the feeling of 'luxurious melancholy' evoked by the ruins of Furness Abbey, Cumbria, during a walking tour in 1794. Her popular novels depicting wild mountain scenery drew on the notion of the 'Picturesque', or roughness and irregularity in nature, developed by the Cumbrian William Gilpin. His illustrated guides to the British Isles were a precursor of the work of early Romantic artists and writers, for whom landscape was a mirror of the human imagination. Similarly, the majestic paintings of ruins and landscapes by J. M. W. Turner (see page 60), often exhibited with accompanying verses, are testimony to his belief that art could match the imaginative power of literature.

***Above**: Detail from a portrait of William Wordsworth (1842) by Benjamin Robert Haydon*

***Left**: The kitchen (now a coffee shop) in Wordworth's house, Cockermouth, looking towards the range*

Among the most celebrated writers associated with the North West was the poet William Wordsworth. In *The Prelude* (published posthumously 1850) Wordsworth recalled how a wren's song in Furness Abbey made him feel he could have 'lived forever there / To hear such music'. As children, he and his sister Dorothy had clambered among the 'mouldering towers' of Brougham Castle and 'gathered with one mind a rich reward / From the far-stretching landscape'. When the French Revolution and the Napoleonic Wars made European travel a dangerous venture, many travellers set out to experience at first hand the scenery of Wordsworth's poetry, and perhaps even to meet the poet himself.

The poet and philosopher Samuel Taylor Coleridge moved to the Lake District in 1800 to work more closely with

Wordsworth. Their collaborative *Lyrical Ballads*, a seminal work of the early Romantic movement, argued against the Classical poetic forms and subject-matter of eighteenth-century writers in favour of the importance of ordinary diction, human imagination and individual experience. They were soon joined by the poet Robert Southey. The journalist Thomas De Quincey, who had met Wordsworth and Coleridge at Oxford, settled in Wordsworth's former cottage in Grasmere, where he wrote *Confessions of an English Opium Eater* (1822) and *Recollections of the Lake Poets* (1834–9).

John Ruskin (1886) by Theodore Blake Wirgman

Wordsworth's poetry also inspired the nineteenth century art critic and moralist John Ruskin, who lived for many years by Coniston Lake. His appreciation of the landscape and vernacular architecture found expression in works such as *The Seven Lamps of Architecture* (1849). During the same period, the novelist Elizabeth Gaskell was a keen observer, in works such as *North and South* (1855), of life in the countryside as well as in the emerging industrial landscape around Manchester.

The landscape of the North West has also appeared in children's literature. The painter and writer Beatrix Potter spent many summers painting in the Lake District, later moving there, to a farm in Sawtry. She used details of her paintings in the illustrations for her books – *The Tale of Peter Rabbit* was the first to be published in 1902 – which have delighted children for generations. The Lakeland landscape is depicted again in *Swallows and Amazons* (1930) and other adventure stories by Arthur Ransome, and in the *Postman Pat* books by the Cumbrian writer John Cunliffe.

Above: *Elizabeth Gaskell (1851) by George Richmond*

Right: *Beatrix Potter (1938) by Delmar Banner*

CASTLERIGG STONE CIRCLE

Above and opposite left: Views of the stone circle with the mountains beyond

There are few stone circles in Britain in such a dramatic setting as that of Castlerigg, which overlooks the Thirlmere Valley with the mountains of High Seat and Helvellyn as a backdrop. It is not just its location that makes this one of the most important British stone circles; considered to have been constructed about 3000 BC, it is potentially one of the earliest in the country. Taken into guardianship in 1883, it was also one of the first monuments in the country to be recommended for preservation by the state.

Although there are more than 300 stone circles in Britain, the great majority of them are Bronze Age burial monuments (dating from approximately 2000–800 BC) containing cremations in central pits or beneath small central cairns. By contrast, their Neolithic forebears, such as Castlerigg, Swinside in the southern part of the Lake District, and Long Meg and her Daughters in the Eden Valley, do not contain formal burials.

The Neolithic stone circles also differ from those of the later Bronze Age in their generally larger size and often flattened circular shape – as is found at Castlerigg – comprising an open circle of many large stones. Castlerigg is about 97 1/2 ft (30 m) in diameter, and formerly comprised forty-two stones; there are now only thirty-eight stones, which vary in height from 3 1/4 ft (1 m) to 7 1/2 ft (2.3 m).

Neolithic stone circles typically have an entrance and at least one outlying stone. The entrance at

Castlerigg, on the north side of the circle, is flanked by two massive upright stones, and the outlier is presently to the west-south-west of the stone circle, on the west side of the field adjacent to a stile; this stone has been moved from its original position. It has been suggested that such outlying stones had astronomical significance – alignments with planets or stars – although examination of those in early stone circles elsewhere in Britain has shown that there are no consistent orientations for them. One of the more unusual features of Castlerigg is a rectangle of standing stones within the circle; there is only one other comparable example, at the Cockpit, an open stone circle at Askham Fell, near Ullswater.

Castlerigg has not been extensively excavated, and it is therefore not known exactly what might be preserved beneath the surface. Three Neolithic stone axes originating from nearby Great Langdale were recovered from the site in the nineteenth century, and similar finds have been made at other Neolithic stone circles. The precise function of these early circles is not known, but their importance possibly centred on their large internal areas with their formalised entrances. Sites such as Castlerigg were undoubtedly important meeting places for the scattered Neolithic communities, but whether as trading places or as religious centres, or even both, is not known.

One of the stones flanking the entrance to the stone circle

1/2 mile E of Keswick
OS Map 90; ref NY 293236

History

The fifteenth-century pele tower is all that remains of the substantial medieval manor house of Clifton Hall. Demolished in the early nineteenth century to make way for the existing farmhouse, the hall was constructed in the late fourteenth century by the Engaine family. On the death of Eleanor, the sole Engaine heiress, in 1412 the house passed to her son from her first marriage to William Wybergh of St Bees and thus became the property of the Wybergh family.

Clifton Hall remained in the hands of the Wyberghs until the late nineteenth century, although their ownership came under threat in 1652 when Thomas Wybergh's estates were ordered to be sold owing to his support for the Royalists in the Civil War. His family were lucky enough to remain in their home, despite financial difficulties and a legal dispute over ownership of the remainder of the estate. There was more trouble during the Jacobite risings: in 1715 William Wybergh was kidnapped by Scottish soldiers and, on 17 December 1745, the building was occupied and plundered shortly before the Battle of Clifton Moor, the last military engagement fought on English soil.

However, it was practicality and convenience rather than warfare that eventually led to the destruction of Clifton manor house. By the early 1800s the H-plan building with its central hall range and two cross wings

Clifton Hall

A Roman cornelian engraved gem found possibly at the fort at Hardknott

were offices for administration and record-keeping. To the left of the headquarters building was the commander's residence; normally a large house with a courtyard – as befitted his status – at Hardknott this was left unfinished or possibly made into a smaller residence, reflecting the intermittent use of this fort. To the right are the granaries, roofed as a single building. The floors were raised on piers to allow free circulation of air and to reduce the risk of infestation by vermin. The outer walls were buttressed for support against the weight of the roof, while the entrances had raised platforms onto which the carts carrying grain were unloaded.

The central range of buildings, with the granaries in the foreground

Barracks normally occupied the remainder of the fort; at Hardknott, however, no traces of these remain, although the front of the fort possibly contained barracks of stone and timber. At the rear, building would have been extremely difficult owing to the uneven ground, and the soldiers may have been housed in leather tents, remnants of which have been recovered in excavations. The parade-ground, where the garrison exercised and practised drill manoeuvres, lies on a plateau about 218 yds (200 m) to the east.

History

The fort at Hardknott was established early in the second century AD: a fragmentary inscription, dating from the reign of the Emperor Hadrian (117–38), from the south gate records the garrison as the Fourth Cohort of Dalmatians, from the Balkans. The fort was demilitarised in the late 130s, when the Romans reoccupied southern Scotland, but was regarrisoned under Marcus Aurelius in the 160s; it was finally abandoned very early in the third century. Objects found around the fort suggest that thereafter its ruins offered temporary shelter to passing patrols and travellers.

King Arthur's Round Table is one of a group of prehistoric megalithic sites and burial mounds in this area and is situated very near to Mayburgh Henge. Despite its name, this ancient and mysterious monument has been dated to the late Neolithic period, between about 2000 and 1000 BC. It consists of a low circular platform surrounded by a wide ditch and earthen bank, a layout characteristic of prehistoric henges.

There were originally two entrances to the central area – one on the south east, which still exists, and another to the north west; the latter was destroyed, along with part of the bank and ditch, when the road was constructed. The site was excavated in 1937, when evidence for two standing stones at one entrance was found; these are also shown on a seventeenth-century plan. The exact purpose of the monument remains unknown: it may have been the meeting place for a large prehistoric community, perhaps for trading though possibly also for ritual or ceremonial use. During the excavations a long, shallow trench – perhaps where the dead were cremated – was discovered near the centre of the circular platform.

The site may have acquired its name in the seventeenth century or even earlier, due to its circular form, a revival of interest in Arthurian legends – it was thought to be a location for jousting – or the traditional associations of King Arthur with the North West.

Aerial view of King Arthur's Round Table

Below: *Engraving showing King Arthur's Round Table (left) and another henge, no longer visible*

Located at Eamont Bridge, 1 mile S of Penrith

OS Map 90; ref NY 523284

Despite being situated close to the motorway the impressive prehistoric monument of Mayburgh Henge can be a remarkably peaceful place. Once you pass through the entrance into the henge on the east side the reason for this is clear: the central area, almost 325 ft (100 m) in diameter, is surrounded by an enormous bank, composed of river pebbles and now crowned in places by trees. Some parts of the roughly circular bank are almost 10 ft (3 m) high, creating a vast enclosed space. Although the henge is within 1 1/4 miles (2 km) of the centre of Penrith and within a few hundred yards of the neighbouring monument of King Arthur's Round Table, this

Aerial view of Mayburgh Henge

mysterious monument has remained largely undisturbed.

Unusually for a site of this type there is no surrounding ditch, while the bank is extremely tall. Slightly north west of the centre is a single large standing stone, just short of 10 ft (3 m) high. Originally seven others accompanied this: three more in the centre, forming a square with the fourth, and two pairs flanking the entrance. The other stones were recorded as standing in the eighteenth century. It is thought that they may have been removed to provide building material for either Penrith Castle or Eamont Bridge, although there is no real evidence to support this suggestion. Legend has it that the labourers responsible were cursed for their act of desecration, one going mad and another hanging himself.

Mayburgh Henge probably dates to the end of the Neolithic period or the beginning of the Bronze Age, around 4,500 years ago. The function of such large monuments is not fully understood, although it is thought that they played a role in social or ritual activities, perhaps involving trade or astronomical observations. Over the centuries several artefacts have been discovered within the vicinity of the henge, including a bronze axe, a stone axe and a flint arrowhead, but these shed little light on its probable use.

What is certainly evident from the sheer size of the bank and the effort clearly invested in its construction is that this was a monument of some importance. Its close proximity to the later henge of King Arthur's Round Table, and the surviving records of prehistoric burial mounds in the area, also demonstrate that this was an area of some cultural significance in the later prehistoric period. As part of the millennium celebrations in the year 2000 a large stone monolith was erected nearby, intended to acknowledge the past, present and future importance of the monument.

The standing stone in the middle of the henge

1 mile S of Penrith off A6

OS Map 90; ref NY 519285

History

Now set in a park in the town of Penrith, Penrith Castle was built about 1397 to defend the town from continuing Scottish raids, one of which had burnt down the town in 1345. The castle was built by William Strickland, Bishop of Carlisle, who received licences to crenellate a 'fortalice' (a fortified house) in 1397 and 1399.

After the bishop's death the castle passed into the possession of the Nevilles, lords of the manor of Penrith and one of the most powerful families in England, with extensive landholdings in the north. They were probably responsible for constructing the impressive moat. The family briefly lost possession of the castle in 1460 following the death of Richard Neville at the battle of Wakefield during the Wars of the Roses. It was taken into royal ownership in 1471, and granted by Edward IV to his brother Richard, Duke of Gloucester, who had married Anne Neville. He was governor of Carlisle Castle and Warden of the Western Marches. At Penrith, one of his many northern homes, much of the present layout of buildings in the castle interior dates from his occupation. When he became king, as Richard III, in 1483, he kept control of the castle, but it was then maintained by custodians.

Penrith Castle

View of the castle from the park

Richard's reign was brief: he was deposed by Henry Tudor, who became King Henry VII, in 1485. In the sixteenth century, during the rule of the Tudor dynasty, the castle fell into decay, and the stone was removed to construct other buildings in the town. It was further damaged during the Civil War by a detachment of Parliamentarian soldiers under General Lambert, who had his headquarters here in 1648. During the 1650s the castle was slighted and dismantled. Stables and other buildings were later erected against the walls but were removed after the castle entered state guardianship in 1913.

Description

Built in red sandstone in the form of a compact square, the castle contains ranges of buildings around a courtyard. Most of the curtain wall survives, with the remains of a projecting tower, known as Strickland's Tower, on the north-east side. Under Richard III the defences of the castle entrance were strengthened by the addition of a second tower and outer gatehouse on the north side. The foundations of other buildings added by Richard III survive around the inside of the castle, including the large hall, with adjoining kitchen range with oven and fireplace. There is also a well near the centre of the courtyard.

Opposite Penrith railway station
OS Map 90; ref NY 513299
Park open: 7.30am-9pm in summer; 7.30am-4.30pm in winter

Description

Perched on the south-east tip of Piel Island, the imposing Piel Castle is visible from around Morecambe Bay. The site is dominated by the massive keep, which is enclosed by both an inner and an outer bailey, each bordered by a ditch and set with corner towers. The stone used to construct the castle was taken from the beach, although red sandstone was imported for architectural details.

Opposite: *View of the castle from the shore*

Plan of Piel Castle

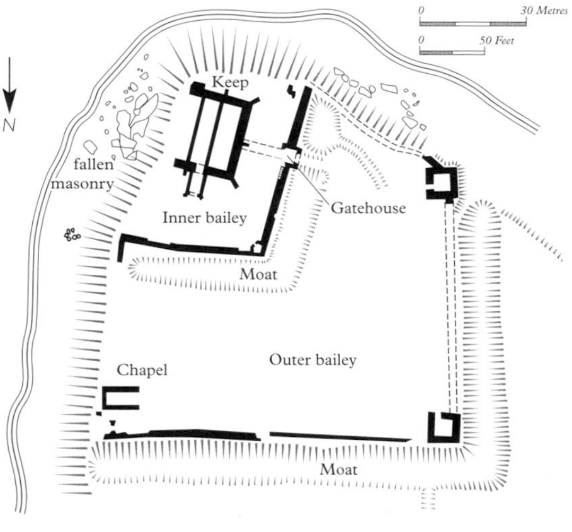

The best place to begin a tour of the castle is at the ruinous, though once ornate, tower that marks the north-east corner of the outer bailey and may have originally formed part of the outer gate. The low structure immediately below it has traditionally been interpreted as the chapel. Walking beside the curtain wall, you will encounter two other simple, two-storeyed towers.

Occupied by the three-storey keep, the inner bailey, entered through the gatehouse in the western wall, is much smaller than the outer. The way into the keep lies on the first floor of the integral two-storey gatehouse. Above the entrance is a worn carved grotesque, usually identified as Salome. The upper floors probably housed the important chambers, with the ground floor being used as storage space. The tower at the south-east corner may have contained private apartments. Unusually the keep has two spine walls, instead of one, dividing it into three parallel sections.

History

Although the large windows on the upper floors of Piel Castle keep give it the appearance of a comfortable residence, it is generally thought that the castle was erected for defensive reasons. In 1327 John Cockerham, Abbot of Furness, was granted a 'licence to crenellate' by Edward III, suggesting that he may have been fortifying an existing building. At this time much of northern England was troubled by Scottish raids, and the monks of Furness wished to establish a place of safety. They probably also wanted to monitor traffic passing through Piel Harbour on its way to their holdings in Ireland and the Isle of Man, and to protect cargoes from the weather, raiders and pirates.

Quarrels over trade (and charges of smuggling) meant that the monks were not always on the best of terms with the king. On 4 June 1487, Lambert Simnel landed on Piel Island from Ireland, with an 8,000-strong army of mercenaries. The son of an Oxford tradesman, he claimed to be the Earl of Warwick and thus rightful heir to the English throne. He marched on London, but was defeated and captured at Newark by Henry VII and his forces.

In 1537, when Furness Abbey was dissolved, the castle became the property of Henry VIII but was left to fall into ruins. The four pilot houses and the pub were built in the late eighteenth century. In 1920 the island was presented by the Duke of Buccleuch to the people of Barrow and District to commemorate those who died in the First World War.

Located on Piel Island, 3 miles SE of Barrow
OS Map 96, ref SD 233636
Access by boat from Roa Island in summer, subject to tides and weather.
Call 01229 835809, 07798 794550 or 07799 7761306

The remains of the bath house at the north-east corner of the Roman fort at Ravenglass

Description

The remains of the bath house at Ravenglass are the most substantial visible evidence of the Roman fort that once stood on this site. They are located beside a metalled track off the modern road just before Ravenglass village. Recent clearance of undergrowth has revealed the site of the fort itself, bounded by at least one defensive ditch, on the other side of the track. The bath house was situated just outside the north-east corner of the fort.

This impressive site comprises some of the tallest Roman structures surviving in northern Britain: doorways and windows, as well as an elegant niche for a bust, can still be made out in the walls. Domestic use of the building in the Middle Ages is the reason why so much has survived. Excavations in the late nineteenth century and survey work in the 1980s indicated that the bath house was a substantial structure extending beyond the present field boundary, as well as to either side of the existing structures. At least two rooms contained underfloor hypocausts (heating systems).

The bath house provided relaxation for the Roman soldiers and for civilians who lived in the settlement outside the fort, which extended here over much of the present field beyond the fence. The building offered facilities for exercise and sport, as well as for swimming and bathing; it was also the obvious place in a Romanised community for people to meet socially.

History

The fort at Ravenglass guarded what was probably a very serviceable harbour. Excavations in the 1970s on the surviving fort platform (between the railway and the sea) indicated that the fort had probably been founded during the reign of the Emperor Hadrian (AD 117–38). However, beneath it, and on a different alignment, was an earlier fort, presumably dating from the first century AD.

The excavations showed that the Hadrianic fort was initially defended by a wall of stacked turfs, but that this had later been strengthened by the addition of a fronting stone wall. Inside the fort, the only buildings excavated were a succession of timber barracks. The most significant find in these was a collection of bone counters, which evidently belonged to some kind of 'war-game'. The barracks appeared to have been in continuous use until the later fourth century when, after destruction by fire (whether deliberate or accidental is unknown), they were rebuilt, using a different method of construction. This suggests that in this period and beyond the fort became the base for a local warlord and his militia after the departure of the Roman army.

One infantry unit of the Roman army is associated with Ravenglass, the First Cohort *Aelia Classica*. 'Aelius' was Hadrian's family name, while 'Classica' is derived from the Latin *classis*, meaning 'fleet', suggesting that the soldiers were recruited from the fleet in Hadrian's time. The most significant evidence for the presence of this unit at Ravenglass was an inscribed bronze certificate of demobilisation belonging to one of the soldiers. That archaeological research is a fortuitous business is shown by the fact that this object was recovered by a dog.

One of the doorways in the bath house

Left: *A reconstruction of the bath house at Wall; that at Ravenglass may have looked similar to this*

¼ mile E of Ravenglass, off minor road leading to A595
OS Map 96; ref NY 088958

History

Shap Abbey was founded in the late twelfth century in a secluded and beautiful valley of the River Lowther, at the foot of the fells. It was one of thirty-two houses in Britain of the Premonstratensian Order of canons. This order, known as the 'White Canons' because of their distinctive white woollen habits, had been founded by St Norbert in Prémontré in northern France in 1120, for those who wished to combine the contemplative life with the active life of a parish priest serving the local community.

The west tower of the church is the dominant feature of the abbey remains

The abbey was established shortly after 1190 by a Westmorland magnate named Thomas, son of Gospatric, originally on land near Kendal. It was a relatively small community, with only about twelve canons governed by an abbot, but it was wealthy, owning lands throughout Westmorland donated by powerful northern families such as the Vieuxponts and the Cliffords. Apart from some Scottish raids causing damage to the property in the fourteenth century, the abbey's history was relatively uneventful. Its most eminent abbot was Richard Redman, who became a canon of Shap during the reign of Henry VI and was elected abbot while still young. During his long rule, from about 1458 to 1505, the abbey prospered. His great ability as an administrator led to his appointment as head of the Premonstratensian Order in England and bishop successively of St Asaph, Exeter and Ely.

During the Dissolution of the Monasteries the last abbot surrendered to the king's men on 14 January 1540, although all the occupants – the abbot and fourteen canons – received pensions. In 1545 the estate was granted to Sir Thomas Wharton and it later passed to the Lowther family. Parts of the abbey were incorporated into farm buildings, but the rest gradually fell into disrepair. The abbey remains were placed by the Lowther Estate in the guardianship of the state in 1948.

Description

Today, access to the abbey is via a late medieval bridge from the car park. Although visitors now enter the site through the west tower of the church, the medieval visitor would not have entered the church directly but would have first gained admission to the abbey precinct through a gatehouse near the tower. The west tower, the most impressive surviving feature, was probably commissioned by Abbot Redman from the same masons who built the west towers at the abbeys of Fountains and Furness. It stands to its original full height except for its parapets. The plan of the rest of the abbey church and buildings around the cloister is still clearly visible. In front of you as you enter the nave of the church from the tower are fragments of a late medieval stone pavement; on each side are traces of incised circles that served to mark the positions taken up by canons as they entered church at end of the Sunday procession. To your right lie the remains of the other abbey buildings around the cloister, including the chapter house, storerooms and infirmary, most of which were built during the thirteenth century.

An early eighteenth-century engraving of Shap Abbey by Samuel Buck

1 1/2 miles W of Shap on the bank of the River Lowther

OS Map 90; ref NY 548153

At the Norman Conquest in 1066 the few dozen monasteries in England were concentrated in the south and midlands.

New monasteries founded in the years immediately after 1066 were mainly in the towns. The first in the North West was St Werburgh's, Chester, founded in 1093 for monks of the Benedictine Order.

By the time St Werburgh's was founded, there was widespread dissatisfaction with the Benedictine and Cluniac Orders: they were thought to be too worldly, with a preoccupation with possessions that was contrary to the monastic ideal. From the late eleventh century new orders with far more rigorous regimes were established and they sought out wild and remote sites. The North West, with its low population and large areas of upland, moor and forest, offered many potential sites for these new foundations.

In 1124 Stephen, Count of Boulogne, founded a monastery at Tulketh in the Ribble Valley for Savigniac monks from Normandy, France. In 1127 they moved to a far more remote site, where they founded the abbey of Furness. In 1147 the Savigniac Order merged with the Cistercians, the most successful of the new orders. Founded in Burgundy in 1098, the Cistercian Order had an austere regime, with an emphasis on manual labour, which they regarded as part of worship. They transformed inhospitable sites through sheer hard work, exploiting whatever resources were available. In the North West they specialised in sheep-farming, selling high-quality wool to merchants in Italy and

Above left: *Head of an abbot of Furness Abbey*
Below: *One of the carved stone corbels at Furness Abbey*

the Low Countries. The monks of Furness also mined the rich iron reserves across the abbey's estates, as well as salt from coastal pans, and traded with Ireland and the Isle of Man.

A medieval depiction of shepherds and sheep

Some of the sites settled by the Cistercians proved too harsh even for such an austere order. Stanlow, founded on the bank of the Mersey in 1172, was so damaged by flooding that in 1296 the monks moved to Whalley in Lancashire. The new abbey was close to that of Sawley, and the two quarrelled incessantly over lands.

A number of new foundations were for canons. As some, such as the Augustinians, served the lay community, their houses were in or close to towns and cities, the first house in the North West being founded at Carlisle in 1122. Others, such as the Premonstratensians, were far closer to the Cistercians in their austerity: Shap Abbey, founded in 1201, is typical of their isolated and remote houses.

Over time the monastic orders gradually became more worldly. The Black Death (1349) adversely affected the Cistercians, who no longer had the manpower to work their estates. Lands were thus increasingly leased out to tenants. However, the monasteries remained popular in the North West, and when Henry VIII attempted to dissolve the smaller houses in 1536 an uprising took place in their support. Nevertheless, all had been swept away by 1540: most were demolished and the stone used for building material, and a few were converted to country houses. Only the two cathedrals of Carlisle and Chester, and a few monastic churches that had passed to the local community, such as Cartmel and Lanercost, were retained for worship.

A medieval farming scene

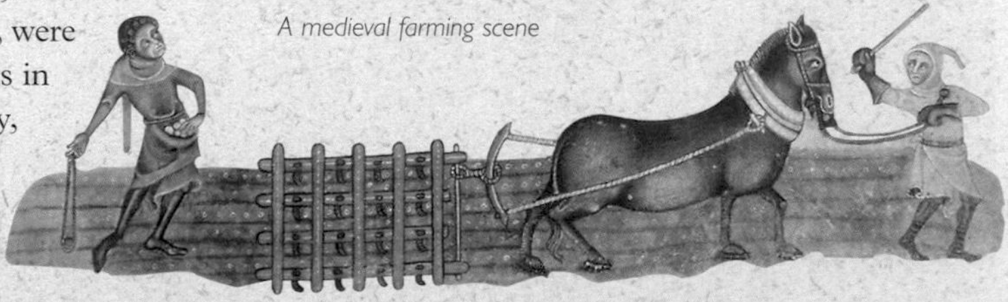

History

This fifteenth-century gatehouse, beside a narrow lane to the south of Wetheral village, is almost all that remains of the Benedictine priory of Wetheral, founded in the early twelfth century when Ranulf Meschin, first Norman lord of Cumberland, gave the manor of Wetheral to the abbot of St Mary's, York. Only a few years earlier, in 1092, William II of England had gained control of the region from the Scots, and had put Meschin, brother of the Earl of Chester, in charge of this strategically important Border area. Wetheral Priory was probably the earliest post-Conquest monastic foundation in this area, and its establishment formed part of the Norman colonisation of northern England.

A cell of the Benedictine abbey of St Mary's in York, Wetheral Priory was a small community, with no more than twelve monks and a prior, and never became fully independent. Nevertheless, it was able to offer hospitality to the future Edward II in 1301 and 1307. It was also an important place of sanctuary in the Border region. Within an area bounded by small stone crosses, wrongdoers could claim freedom from arrest. They were then obliged to toll a bell in the church and to swear to keep the peace before the bailiff of the manor. In 1342 Edward III offered a pardon to those claiming sanctuary here on condition that they fought for him against the Scots.

View of the gatehouse from the lane

One of the ground-floor windows

At the Dissolution of the Monasteries, under Henry VIII, the last prior, Ralf Hartley, signed the deed of surrender in 1538, and he and at least four other monks received an annual pension. The priory's furnishings and other possessions were sold, although the more valuable items, such as church plate, were handed over to the king's receiver. The church and monastic buildings fell into decay, but the gatehouse was preserved by being used as vicarage in the sixteenth and seventeenth centuries, before becoming a hayloft. It passed into state guardianship in 1978.

Description

The gatehouse, constructed of red sandstone, was the original entrance to the priory precinct; beyond it lay an outer court with barns, stables, stores, a bakehouse and a brewhouse and then the church and monastic buildings. Traces of rooflines can be seen on two sides of the gatehouse, indicating that it was originally part of a range of other buildings including a chapel and monastic school. As well as controlling entry to the priory, the gatehouse was a reflection of the status of the monastery in its impressive size and elaborate decoration. Through the gatehouse is the main entrance passage, with a small lodge for the porter alongside, lit by narrow windows at either end. A circular stair leads to domestic chambers on the first and second floors, with larger windows that would have given a good view of approaching visitors. Each floor consists of a hall with a garderobe (latrine) and fireplace, and may have been used by priory officials or as guest lodgings for important visitors and travellers. The floor of the upper chamber does not survive.

In Wetheral village, 6 miles E of Carlisle on B6263
OS Map 86; ref NY 469542
Open
29 Mar-30 Sep: 10am-6pm daily;
1-31 Oct: 10am-5pm daily;
1 Nov-31 Mar: 10am-4pm daily;
closed 24-26 Dec and 1 Jan

LANCASHIRE

Like Cumbria, which borders it to the north, ownership of Lancashire was long disputed: in the early medieval period by rulers of the kingdoms of Mercia and Northumbria, and from the twelfth century between the Crown and nobility. The Dukedom of Lancaster, created in 1351, became one of the most important in England, and the House of Lancaster ruled England from 1399 to 1461. From the eighteenth century the county was at the centre of the Industrial Revolution, with innovations in machinery and engineering developed by Lancashire men such as Samuel Crompton. The manufacture of cotton textiles became the dominant industry, and its importance is reflected in the remaining mill buildings.

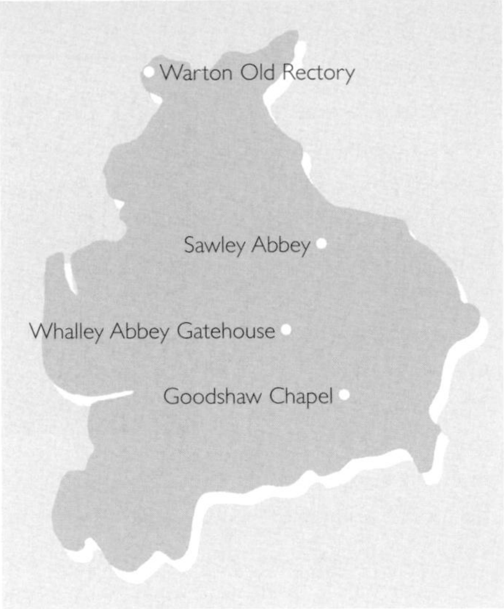

Opposite: *Nineteenth-century tombstone from Goodshaw Chapel graveyard*

Below: *Whalley Abbey Gatehouse*

Left: *Detail from an engraving of Sawley Abbey from* The Monastic Ruins of Yorkshire, *1842, by George Hawkins*

In Affectionate
Remembrance
OF THE LATE
THOMAS PARKINSON,
F CRAWSHAWBOOTH, WHO DIED
April 6th 1864, in the 76th Yea

History

East Lancashire was an early centre of religious dissent in England. In the early seventeenth century the region was noted for its strong dissenting tradition; after 1690, when non-conformists (Christians who did not conform to the Church of England) secured freedom of worship, a multitude of meeting places for their congregations appeared. In the early eighteenth century these were often barns or private houses, but by the 1740s purpose-built chapels were more common. Architecturally the presentation of these buildings was invariably plain and simple, partly to distinguish them from Anglican churches and partly because they were built by the congregations themselves, using local materials and with limited funds.

The Baptists established a meeting at Lumb, east of Goodshaw, in 1742. This soon united with a group of Wesleyans, and in 1760 the combined congregation built a new chapel at Goodshaw, using materials from an older chapel. The pews were reputedly brought across the moor from Lumb on the shoulders of the men. Today Goodshaw Chapel stands beside a narrow lane, with a housing estate down the hill, but in 1760 this was the main Burnley road, with few houses nearby. Such places – accessible from farms and cottages over a wide area – were typical of early nonconformist places of worship.

The congregation grew as the expansion of the textile industry encouraged local population growth.

The exterior of the chapel

Opposite: *One of the monuments in the graveyard*

At the beginning of the nineteenth century the chapel was extended to its present size, but in 1864 a new chapel was built on the main road and this one then saw only occasional use. In the mid-twentieth century the building was no longer in use and by the late 1960s was derelict, but in 1975 it was recognised as a unique survival of an early nonconformist chapel retaining many of its original internal features. It was taken into the guardianship of the Department of the Environment and a full restoration scheme was completed in 1984.

Description

From the outside the building is characteristic of nonconformist chapels of the period, and it was built with gritstones and flagstones from the nearby hillsides. The original walls are those to the north (the back) and the east (the uphill side). The west wall, now covered with protective slates, was once the party wall to an adjoining building where the Sunday school was held. The south front, with the main entrance, was built when the chapel was extended about 1800.

The interior fittings are superbly preserved and give an excellent impression of a small, unpretentious rural chapel over 200 years ago. The box pews, closely packed together, were constructed at the beginning of the nineteenth century. Above them are wooden galleries reached by stone-slabbed staircases. The side galleries are largely original, dating from 1760. On the south side is a larger pew that accommodated the chapel singers, and the communion table; above it is the fine early nineteenth-century pulpit with its staircase and the canopy that functioned as a sounding-board. The graveyard at Goodshaw has a particularly interesting collection of early nineteenth-century gravestones, with moving epitaphs and inscriptions.

In Crawshawbooth, 2 miles N of Rawtenstall, off Goodshaw Avenue off A682
OS Map 103; ref SD 815263
Keykeeper: please call 0161 242 1400 for details

Sawley Abbey was founded in 1146 on land given by William, third Lord Percy. The Percys, Northumberland's greatest family, remained patrons of the abbey for much of its existence. The help of these wealthy benefactors proved invaluable in the 1280s when it seemed likely that the monks would abandon the site: they claimed that poor harvests, marshy ground and the inhospitable climate made life at Sawley untenable. In response, Maud de Percy, Countess of Warwick, gave valuable lands and churches at Rimington (near Barnoldswick), Ilkley, Gargrave and Tadcaster. With this new endowment the monks stayed put.

Plan of the church at Sawley Abbey

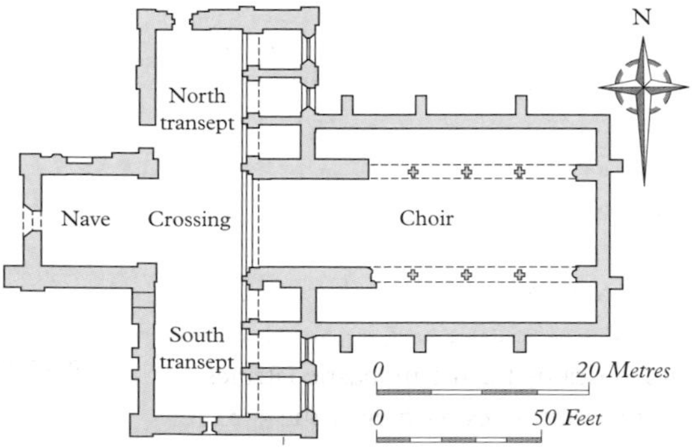

Their problems, though, did not disappear. In 1296 Stanlaw Abbey in Cheshire was refounded at Whalley, nine miles from Sawley, and the two Cistercian houses immediately quarrelled. Their lands adjoined and they squabbled over grain supplies and fishing rights in the River Ribble. The feuding officially ended in 1305, but the monks of Sawley, the senior foundation, continued to feel aggrieved. Sawley was considerably poorer than Whalley: it was impoverished by litigation, the 'cruel and inhuman spoliation' that accompanied Scottish raids about 1320, and the expense of providing board and lodging to travellers – unlike many Cistercian houses it lay on a busy main road.

In spring 1536 Sawley surrendered during Henry VIII's Dissolution of the Monasteries. However, that autumn, during the northern rising known as the Pilgrimage of Grace, the abbey was restored under a new abbot, William Trafford. The rebellion failed and Trafford was hanged at Lancaster in March 1537 and the abbey immediately plundered of its valuables. During the following three centuries all the high-quality stone was taken and reused in neighbouring farms and cottages, and many of the abbey buildings disappeared. In 1848 the first archaeological investigation of the ruins was undertaken, and during the twentieth century the site was taken into the care of the state, cleared of debris and conserved.

The poverty of the abbey was probably the reason for its strangest feature: its extremely short nave, still clearly visible today. It is known that it was intended to be full length because the cloister, on the south side of the church, was built to normal size, but probably a lack of money meant that the nave was never finished. In contrast, the chancel at the east end is exceptionally wide because new aisles were constructed to the north and south in the early sixteenth century, when more funds were available and ambitious rebuilding was fashionable. The result was a church unlike that of any other Cistercian abbey.

Another impressive feature visible today is the well-preserved night stair in the south transept, used by the monks to walk from the now-vanished first-floor dormitory down into the church for night-time services. On the west side of the cloister is the substantial ruin of the abbot's lodgings: this was converted to a cottage after 1537, and the great fireplaces and ovens date from this later period. Note, too, the stone-lined drains for the monastic latrines at the south-west corner of the site.

A stone-lined drain

Left: *View across the abbey ruins*

At Sawley,
3½ miles N of Clitheroe off A59
OS Map 103; ref SD 778464
Open
29 Mar-30 Sep: 10am-6pm daily;
1-31 Oct: 10am-5pm daily;
1 Nov-31 Mar: 10am-4pm daily

History

Warton Old Rectory is a rare surviving example of a large medieval stone dwelling-house. It was not only a home for the rector of the local church, which was founded in the twelfth century or earlier, but was also a manor where courts were held. It became one of the wealthiest rectories in the diocese of York. By the end of the twelfth century patronage determining the appointment of priests to the position of rector was held by Marmaduke de Thweng. Two of his younger sons, both priests, inherited his property when their elder brother died childless; they were probably responsible for building the rectory in the early fourteenth century. Control of the appointment of rectors was contested between the de Thweng family and the monarch, as Duke of Lancaster, until the sixteenth century.

The arched entrance doorway

Unlike monastic houses the rectory was not directly affected by the Dissolution of the Monasteries in the sixteenth century. It was nevertheless abandoned at an unknown date and is known to have been a ruin by 1721. The north end of the building was occupied as a cottage until well into the twentieth century, while the site of the medieval hall was roofless. After the site came into the guardianship of the state in 1971 later additions to the rectory were removed, leaving only the medieval parts visible.

View of the rectory from the north east

Description

The rectory is set back from the main street of Warton, opposite the parish church. The entrance, as today, was on the west side, through a pointed archway, which may have had a porch. The layout of the rectory was typical of many important medieval houses: the entrance led into a passage screening a great hall to the right (south) from service rooms to the left (north). The hall was lit by windows on the east and west walls and by a quatrefoil window, below which was a dais. This is where the rector, as befitting his importance, would have sat at meal times and when the court was in session. In the south-west corner of the great hall is a doorway that led to a two-storey building (now part of the modern vicarage); as indicated by a large traceried window, there was possibly a private chapel on the first floor.

The doorways off the other side of the entrance passage led to a buttery, a pantry and a passage through which food would have been brought from a kitchen. At the far end of the entrance passage, directly opposite the entrance, was another door giving access through a porch into the garden. A fourth doorway led to a first-floor chamber with a fireplace, while an annex with a garderobe (latrine) was located to the north of the service block. A pair of cruck timbers removed when the service end of the rectory was stripped of later accretions is now fixed to the modern boundary wall.

At Warton, 1 mile N of Carnforth on minor road off A6
OS Map 97; ref SD 499723
Open 29 Mar-30 Sep: 10am-6pm daily; 1-31 Oct: 10am-5pm daily; 1 Nov-31 Mar: 10am-4pm daily; closed 24-26 Dec and 1 Jan

The great textile mills of the North West are among the region's most distinctive historic buildings. They dominate the urban landscape of east Lancashire and Greater Manchester, and parts of inner Manchester itself, the 'cottonopolis' of the Industrial Revolution.

Cloth has long been a key product of the North West, but the earliest 'factories' for textiles were built only in the eighteenth century. Among notable examples are the important water-powered mills in Derbyshire, now within a World Heritage Site. The invention of the spinning mule – an early form of machine for spinning thread – by Samuel Crompton of Bolton in the late eighteenth century prompted the expansion of the industry. By the 1770s spinning mills were being built in Manchester, to supply the increasing demand for cotton from the growing home market, and from the expanding British empire overseas. With the rapidly developing port of Liverpool close by, importing the raw cotton from the colonies and exporting the finished cloth all over the world, Manchester was well placed to meet this need.

From about 1780 the development of the steam engine allowed larger spinning mills to be built. The greatest concentration of these was in Ancoats, on the northern side of Manchester, but new mills were also built in many other towns in Lancashire. A growing network of canals and, later, railways linked the manufacturing towns

Above: *A wooden bobbin*

Left: *A nineteenth-century engraving of a cotton mill*

with the ports and with the collieries that provided fuel for the engines.

Mill technology developed throughout the nineteenth century. Inventions such as power looms allowed production to expand, while advances in construction enabled larger, fireproof mills to be built. As well as being the leading manufacturing town, Manchester became the centre for trade in cotton textiles, with large numbers of warehouses, where cloth could be stored and packed, and samples shown to prospective customers. Converted to new uses, they still line the streets, in particular Princess Street, of the city centre.

A sample of Victorian cotton textile made in Lancashire

In the 1860s the industry suffered recession as a result of the American Civil War (1861–5), which cut off the largest suppliers of raw cotton, the southern states. However, it recovered within a few years and until the First World War enjoyed a boom. Large numbers of electrically powered cotton mills were built in the early twentieth century, many of them of enormous size, and in extravagant designs by specialist architects.

Cotton was not the only textile to be woven in the North West. Macclesfield was a major centre for silk weaving, while flax was processed into linen cloth in Manchester, Bolton and Preston. The textile industries drew on support from a whole range of others – the region's engineering industry owes its origin largely to the demand for mill machinery. The huge numbers of bobbins required for thread were supplied by firms in the Lake District, and the processes involved in bobbin manufacture can still be seen at Stott Park Bobbin Mill.

Since the Second World War cheap imports of cloth have undermined the English cotton industry, and few of the mills now produce textiles. Many have been demolished, but others have been saved by conversion to new use, helping to preserve the regional character.

View of the gatehouse from the lane

Whalley Abbey *by J. M. W. Turner*

Whalley Abbey, second richest of Lancashire's monasteries, was founded in 1296, when the monks of Stanlaw moved there from their flood-prone site on the Cheshire shore of the River Mersey near Ellesmere Port. Whalley was chosen as their new home because the de Lacy family, Earls of Lincoln and patrons of Stanlaw, held extensive estates in the area. Work soon began on a fine new church and a complex of domestic ranges and outbuildings, the construction of which spanned almost the entire fourteenth century.

The abbey prospered by exploiting its considerable resources – stone, coal, iron, sheep and cattle pastures, fisheries, woollen mills and arable land. According to the historian Owen Ashmore the last abbot, John Paslew, 'not only lived like a lord, but also travelled like one'. But this wealth and status could not save the abbey, or Paslew. In 1536, during the early stages of Henry VIII's Dissolution of the Monasteries, Whalley was caught up in the Pilgrimage of Grace, the northern rebellion against the king. Paslew did not participate but he did refuse to take the compulsory oath of allegiance and was executed, with two of his fellow monks, at Lancaster in March 1537. The abbey was seized by the Crown and in 1553 was bought by Richard Assheton of Lever, near Bolton. Its buildings (apart from the church, of which very little remains) were converted into a large and imposing private house, much of which is now used as a conference centre.

Most monasteries were demarcated by gatehouses that prevented access by any except authorised visitors, allowed the gatekeeper to keep a close watch on traffic and provided basic defence in times of military and political insecurity. At Whalley, as at other monasteries, there was a steady stream of beggars and poor travellers seeking food or help, which the monks could not readily deny. Thus, the gatehouse was also the place where alms were dispensed and food and drink given to the poor.

Today the north-west gatehouse at Whalley Abbey spans a narrow lane, but this was originally the main route northwards up the Ribble Valley. This explains the imposing scale and impressive architecture of the building, which was one of the main entrances to a monastic precinct that covered over 200 acres. The two-storey gatehouse is the oldest of the abbey buildings, constructed between 1296 and 1310 when the new monastery was being established. It has a vaulted ceiling, and halfway along is a cross-wall, with two doorways, one for wheeled vehicles and horses, the other, smaller, one for pedestrians. The upper floor comprised a large and airy room, with three three-light traceried windows on each side (best viewed from the grassed enclosure on the north side), which was probably used as a chapel for guests and visitors to the abbey. On the south side of the building was a guesthouse (now demolished) for visitors – in 1536 it had nine bedrooms, with fourteen feather beds – and on the north side were lodgings for the vicar of Whalley.

The gatehouse from the north

Whalley, 6 miles NE of Blackburn on minor road off A59
OS Map 103; ref SD 730360

Six English Heritage sites in the North West are staffed; each has a separate guidebook, which can be purchased at the gift shop or through mail order. These sites charge an admission fee, although admission is free to members of English Heritage (see inside back cover). Further details of admission charges, access and opening times for these sites are given in the *English Heritage Members' and Visitors' Handbook* (product code: 20000), also available through mail order.

To place an order for the *Handbook,* or for a guidebook for any of the following sites, please contact:

English Heritage Postal Sales
c/o Gillards, Trident Works,
Temple Cloud, Bristol BS39 5AZ

Tel: 01761 452966 Fax: 01761 453408
E-mail: ehsales@gillards.com

Please always quote the product code for the publication you are ordering.

BEESTON CASTLE

CHESHIRE

The ruin of medieval Beeston Castle stands on a rocky summit high above the Cheshire plain, with splendid views of the Pennines in the east to the Welsh mountains in the west. Recent archaeological excavations have indicated that there was a Bronze Age community on the site about 800 BC, and a hill fort developed during the Iron Age. The castle, on the site of this fort, dates from 1225 when it was built by Ranulf, the sixth Earl of Chester, following his return from the Crusades. The castle was seized by Henry III in 1237 and it remained in royal ownership until the sixteenth century. It was refortified during

the Civil War, when the Royalist garrison was besieged by Parliamentary forces, and finally surrendered in 1646, when its defences were largely demolished.

Product code: **04100** Price: **£2.95**

BROUGHAM CASTLE

CUMBRIA

Brougham Castle was built in the early thirteenth century on the site of a Roman fort, in a strategic position by the crossing of the River Eamont and controlling nearby crossroads. Like Brough Castle (see pages 21–3), Brougham was held by the same two families – the Vieuxponts and the Cliffords – throughout much of its history. Owing to its location the castle was strategically important during the Anglo-Scottish wars and the Wars of the Roses. Its function as a military stronghold diminished after the medieval period and the castle was later neglected, especially when it was owned by George Clifford, Earl of Cumberland, who preferred to spend much of his time at the court of Elizabeth I. His daughter, Lady Anne Clifford, the most famous member of the family, later restored and developed

the castle, where she died in 1676. In the eighteenth century the castle fell into ruin, yet proved a source of inspiration for the poet William Wordsworth.

Product code: **04757** Price: **£2.25**

CARLISLE CASTLE

CUMBRIA

Carlisle Castle has seen over 800 years of continuous military use. Frequently raided by the Scots, the castle commanded the western end of the Anglo-Scottish border in the low-lying land surrounding the Solway. Often the scene of turbulent conflict, the castle was besieged on many occasions and was even held by the Scots for several years. In the twelfth-century keep visitors can see the wall-carvings of prisoners incarcerated by Richard of Gloucester,

Warden of the West March, who conducted many hard-fought campaigns against the Scots before seizing the English throne as Richard III in 1483. Many other prisoners followed: it was here that Mary, Queen of Scots, was held in 1568 following her abdication from the Scottish throne, and that many supporters of Bonnie Prince Charlie's Jacobite rising of 1745 were led out to be hanged by the Duke of Cumberland.

Product code: **03791** Price: **£2.95**

FURNESS ABBEY
CUMBRIA

Set in the beautiful Vale of Nightshade are the extensive red sandstone ruins of Furness Abbey, which was founded by Stephen, later King of England, in 1123. The abbey first belonged to the Order of Savigny, and, after 1147, to the much larger and more powerful Cistercian Order. In its heyday Furness knew prosperity on a huge scale, and, by the time of the Dissolution of the Monasteries in the 1530s, it was the second richest Cistercian abbey in England after Fountains. The abbey's wealth and importance are reflected in the quality of the impressive remains. After the Dissolution, it passed through a succession of owners, but fell into decline. From the early nineteenth century – and especially after the construction of the Furness railway, which opened in 1847 – it became a popular visitor attraction.

Product code: **03518** Price: **£2.50**

LANERCOST PRIORY

CUMBRIA

This twelfth-century Augustinian priory, situated near the Scottish border, has a rich and diverse history. Founded by the Vaux family and consecrated in 1169, the

priory enjoyed relative tranquillity as a monastic house until the Anglo-Scottish wars in the fourteenth century. It was one of the first religious houses to be dissolved during the reign of Henry VIII and was granted to the Dacre family. It remained home to this powerful local family until the eighteenth century, after which it fell into ruin. The ruined church contains some fine tombs, including that of Sir Thomas Dacre, who fought at the Battle of Flodden and was created a Knight of the Garter.

Product code: **04435** Price: **£0.30**

STOTT PARK BOBBIN MILL

CUMBRIA

Situated on the western side of Lake Windermere, near the village of Finsthwaite, Stott Park Bobbin Mill is a unique and important monument. Built in 1835, the mill produced the wooden bobbins vital to the spinning and weaving industries of Lancashire. It was worked continuously until 1971, surviving far longer than many other mills. The mill buildings and machinery are predominantly Victorian, and little changed for over 100 years.

Product code: **00009** Price: **£2.25**

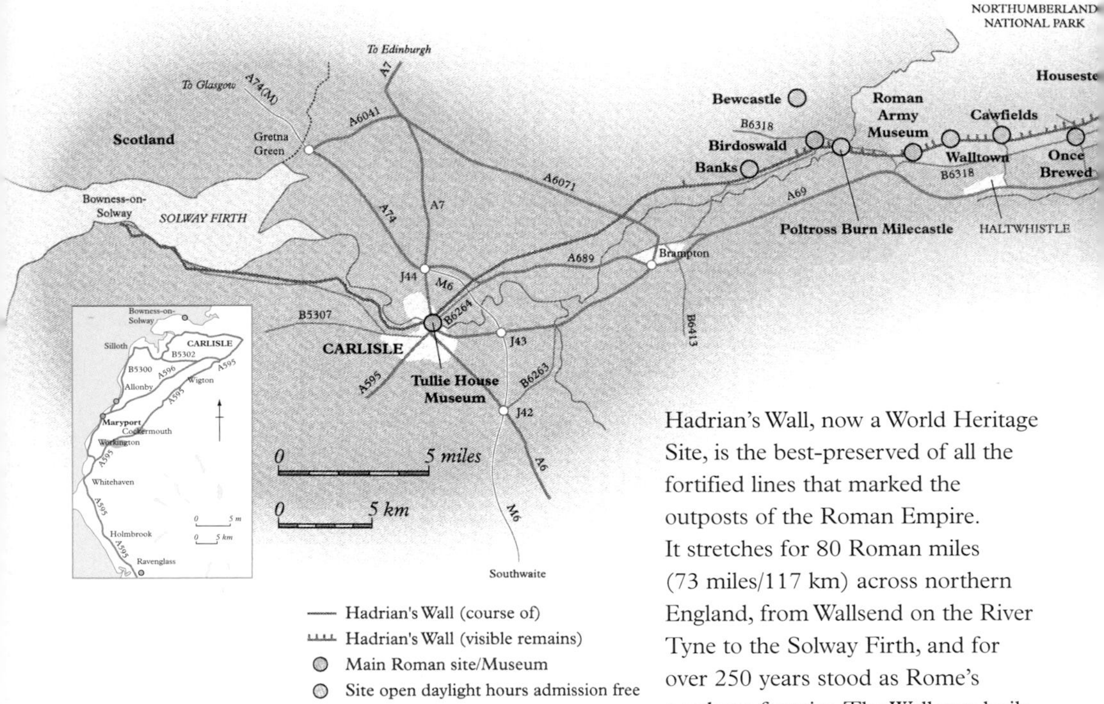

Hadrian's Wall, now a World Heritage Site, is the best-preserved of all the fortified lines that marked the outposts of the Roman Empire. It stretches for 80 Roman miles (73 miles/117 km) across northern England, from Wallsend on the River Tyne to the Solway Firth, and for over 250 years stood as Rome's northern frontier. The Wall was built by order of the Emperor Hadrian, who came to Britain in AD 122, and was intended, as his biographer noted, 'to separate the Romans and

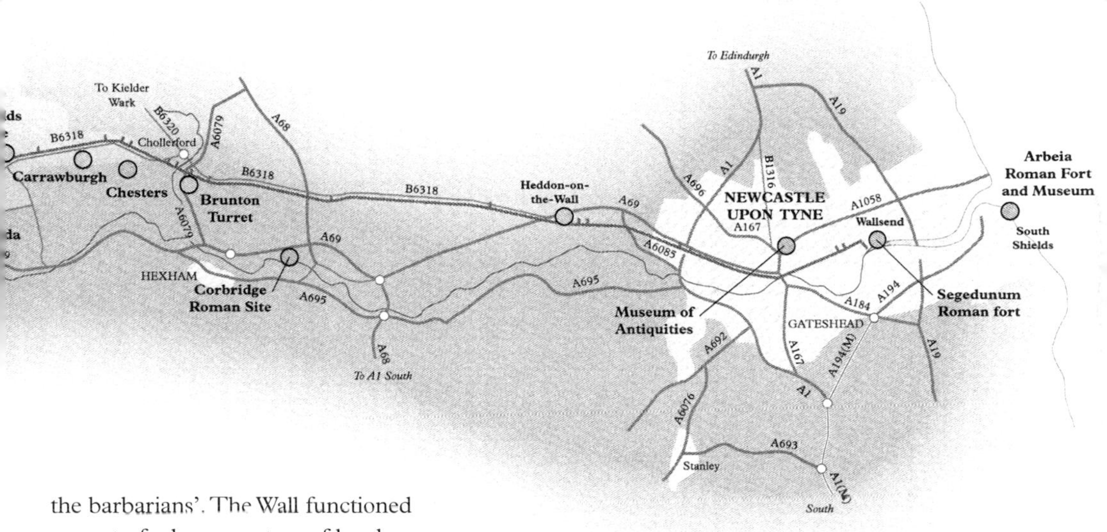

the barbarians'. The Wall functioned as part of a larger system of border defences, and hence not only can the Wall itself be seen today, but also the remains of small forts a mile apart (known as milecastles), turrets and larger forts. At the western end of the Wall these include Birdoswald Roman Fort, Banks East Turret, Pike Hill Signal Turret and Poltross Burn Milecastle. Museums, visitor centres and reconstructions also provide a wealth of information about life along the Wall in Roman times.

For further information please telephone 01434 322002 or visit the website at **www.hadrians-wall.org.**

A full-colour souvenir guide to Hadrian's Wall (product code: 03870; price: £2.95) is available from the address given on page 62.

INDEX

INDEX

FURTHER READING

CHESHIRE

Chester Castle

H. M. Colvin, *History of the King's Works*, 1963, vol. 2, pp 607–12

P. Ellis and others, *Excavations at Chester, Chester Castle: the Seventeenth-century Armoury and Mint. Excavation and Building Recording in the Inner Ward 1979–82*, 1996 (*Chester Archaeology Excavation Survey Report*, no.10)

Chester Roman Amphitheatre

F. H. Thompson, 'The Excavation of the Roman Amphitheatre at Chester', *Archaeologia*, 105, 1976, pp 127–239

Sandbach Crosses

J. Hawkes, *The Sandbach Crosses*, 2002

A. Rimmer, *Ancient Stone Crosses of England*, 1973

P. Timmis Smith, *The Glory of the Saxon Crosses at Sandbach, Cheshire: the Sepulchral Monument of King Egbert with its Picture Language Explained*, 1968

CUMBRIA

Ambleside Roman Fort

R. H. Leech, 'The Roman Fort and Vicus at Ambleside', *Transactions of the Cumberland and Westmorland Archaeological and Antiquarian Society*, 93, 1993, pp 77–95

S. Mann and A. Dunwell, 'An Interim Note on Further Discoveries in the Roman Vicus at Ambleside', *Transactions of the Cumberland and Westmorland Archaeological and Antiquarian Society*, 95, 1995, pp 79–83

D. C. A. Shotter, 'Three Roman Forts in the Lake District', *Archaeological Journal*, 155, 1998, pp 338–51

Brough Castle

Further information on Brough Castle can be found in the English Heritage guidebook to Brougham Castle by H. Summerson, 1999

Castlerigg Stone Circle

T. Clare, *Archaeological Sites of the Lake District*, 1981

Archaeological Journal, 155, 1998, pp 368–9

Clifton Hall

J. F. Curwen, *The Castles and Fortified Towers of Cumberland, Westmorland and Lancashire North-of-the Sands*

G. Fairclough, 'Clifton Hall Excavations', *Transactions of the Cumberland and Westmorland Archaeological and Antiquarian Society*, 80, 1980

Countess Pillar

R. T. Spence, *Lady Anne Clifford*, 1997

Hardknott Roman Fort

D. Charlesworth, 'The Granaries at Hardknott Castle', *Transactions of the Cumberland and Westmorland Archaeological and Antiquarian Society*, 63, 1963, pp 148–52

R. G. Collingwood, 'Hardknott Castle', *Transactions of the Cumberland and Westmorland Archaeological and Antiquarian Society*, 28, 1928, pp 314–52

C. W. Dymond, 'The Roman Fort at Hardknott, known as Hardknott Castle', *Transactions of the Cumberland and Westmorland Archaeological and Antiquarian Society*, 12, 1892–3, pp 375–439

D. C. A. Shotter, 'Three Roman Forts in the Lake District', *Archaeological Journal*, 155, 1998, pp 338–51

R. P. Wright, 'A Hadrianic Building-Inscription from Hardknott', *Transactions of the Cumberland and Westmorland Archaeological and Antiquarian Society*, 65, 1965, pp 169–75

King Arthur's Round Table

T. Clare, in *Archaeological Journal*, 155, 1998

R. Bradley and P. Topping, in *Proceedings of the Prehistoric Society*, vol. 58, 1992; vol. 60, 1994

Mayburgh Henge

T. Clare, in *Archaeological Journal*, 155, 1998

P. Topping, in *Proceedings of the Prehistoric Society*, 58, 1992

Penrith Castle

D. Perriam and J. Robinson, *The Medieval Fortified Buildings of Cumbria*, 1998, pp 212–13 (with further reading)

FURTHER READING

Piel Castle

Further information on Piel Castle is given in the English Heritage guidebook to Furness Abbey, by S. Harrison, J. Wood and R. Newman, 1998

Ravenglass Roman Bath House

E. B. Birley, 'The Roman Fort at Ravenglass', *Transactions of the Cumberland and Westmorland Archaeological and Antiquarian Society*, 58, 1958, pp 14–30

M. L. Brann, 'A Survey of Walls Castle, Ravenglass, Cumbria', *Transactions of the Cumberland and Westmorland Archaeological and Antiquarian Society*, 85, 1985, pp 81–5

R. G. Collingwood, 'Roman Ravenglass', *Transactions of the Cumberland and Westmorland Archaeological and Antiquarian Society*, 28, 1928, pp 353–66

P. A. Holder, 'A Roman Military Diploma from Ravenglass, Cumbria', *Bulletin of the John Rylands Library*, 79, 1997, 3–41

D. C. A. Shotter, 'Three Roman Forts in the Lake District', *Archaeological Journal*, 155, 1998, pp 338–51

Shap Abbey

H. M. Colvin and R. Gilyard-Beer, *Shap Abbey*, 1963

Royal Commission on Historical Monuments, *Westmorland*, 1936

Articles in *Cumberland and Westmorland Transactions*, 10, 1889; *Archaeologia*, 73, 1922; *Medieval Archaeology*, 1, 1957

Wetheral Priory Gatehouse

J. E. Prescott (ed.), *The Register of the Priory of Wetheral*, 1897, with introduction on the history of Wetheral

LANCASHIRE

Goodshaw Chapel

V. Brandon and S. Johnson, 'The Old Baptist Chapel, Goodshaw Chapel, Rawtenstall, Lancs', *The Antiquaries Journal*, 66, pt 2, 1986

Warton Old Rectory

J. Kestell Floyer, 'The Old Rectory House and Rectory of Warton', *Transactions of the Historic Society of Lancashire and Cheshire*, 57 (new series vol. 21), 1906

'Preserving the Legacy'

J. and J. Bennett (eds.), *A Guide to the Industrial Archaeology of Cumbria*, 1993

M. Davies-Shiel and J. Marshall, *Industrial Archaeology of the Lake Counties*, 1969

R. McNeil and M. Nevell, *A Guide to the Industrial Archaeology of Greater Manchester*, 2000

North West England in Roman Times

D. J. Breeze, *The Northern Frontiers of Roman Britain*, 1982

D. C. A. Shotter, *Romans and Britons in North-west England*, 1997 (2nd edn)

D. C. A. Shotter, 'The Roman Conquest of the North West', *Transactions of the Cumberland and Westmorland Archaeological and Antiquarian Society*, 100, 2000, pp 33–53

J. Southworth, *Walking the Roman Roads of Cumbria*, 1985, esp pp 117–52

'The Far-stretching Landscape'

W. H. Auden and N. H. Pearson (eds.), *The Portable Romantic Poets*, 1950

D. Blayney Brown, *Romanticism*, 2001

W. Vaughan, *Romanticism and Art*, 1995

D. Wright (ed.), *English Romantic Verse*, 1968

'Lanterns Burning in a Dark Place'

M. Aston, *Monasteries in the Landscape*, 2000

J. Patrick Greene, *Medieval Monasteries*, 1992

C. Platt, *The Abbeys and Priories of Medieval England*, 1984

D. Robinson (ed.), *The Cistercian Abbeys of Britain: Far from the Concourse of Men*, 1998

'Palaces of Industry'

A.Calladine and J. Fricker, *East Cheshire Textile Mills*, 1993

M. Williams with D. Farnie, *Cotton Mills in Greater Manchester*, 1992

Acknowledgements

English Heritage thanks the many individuals and organisations who helped in putting this book together, especially all our contributors for their insights into the heritage of the North West, and the following people for their assistance and advice: Mr W. S. Anderson, Whalley Abbey Council; Dr Peter Carrington, Chester City Council; Kathy Fishwick and the Rossendale Civic Trust; Dr Jane Hawkes, University of York; Robert Maxwell, National Trust; John Miller, Heritage Trust for the North West; and Eileen Wilshaw, Chester City Council. Sincere thanks are also due to the local communities within which these monuments are located for their continual support and assistance.

The editor would like to thank the English Heritage North West region, in particular Malcolm Cooper, Richard Polley, Marion Barter, Andrew Davison, David Sherlock and Joanne Balmforth, for their invaluable help, encouragement and advice; Paul Austen for assistance in compiling the Hadrian's Wall spread; Pauline Hull for creating and developing the outstanding and innovative design; Richard Jones for help on production; Jeanette Cole for membership information; Katie Myers for marketing; John Clarke for help on interpretation; and Val Horsler and the EH Publications team.

A number of the sites in this book are in the guardianship of English Heritage but managed by other organisations, as follows: Ambleside Roman Fort (National Trust); Chester Castle: Agricola Tower and Castle Walls (Chester City Council); Chester Roman Amphitheatre (Chester City Council); Hardknott Roman Fort (National Trust); Ravenglass Roman Bath House (Lake District National Park); Sawley Abbey (Heritage Trust for the North West); Shap Abbey (Lake District National Park); Warton Old Rectory (Heritage Trust for the North West); Whalley Abbey Gatehouse (Whalley Abbey Council); Castlerigg Stone Circle is owned by the National Trust and managed by English Heritage.

Useful websites relating to the North West

www.english-heritage.org.uk
(English Heritage)

www.hadrians-wall.org
(Hadrian's Wall Tourism Partnership)

www.cheshire.gov.uk/tourism
(Cheshire Tourism links)

www.chestercc.gov.uk
(Chester City Council)

www.cumbria-the-lake-district.co.uk
(Cumbria Tourist Board)

www.htnw.co.uk
(Heritage Trust for the North West)

www.lake-district.gov.uk
(Lake District National Park Authority)

www.lancaster.ac.uk
(Lancaster University)

www.nationaltrust.org.uk
(National Trust)

www.visitnorthwest.com
(North West Tourist Board)